D0581746

POCKET

SINGLE LIFE

WISDOM

A celebration of the self-partnered

Hardie Grant

BOOKS

CONTENTS

"Single and ready to mingle."

INTRODUCTION

"The right ONE is just around the corner."

"As soon as you stop looking, you'll meet someone."

For all the single guys and gals out there, these are the things often heard when asked that inevitable question, "So are you seeing anyone?"

Well, not anymore! This little book is filled with real, meaningful, sassy quotes on just how great the single life really is, from people who've been there and really know. So, sit back and prepare yourself for inspiration on your ultimate relationship: YOU!

1

STRONG, SEXY AND SINGLE

"I've been super, super single for two years… I've been having way too much fun being on my own. It sucked for the first year, I was like, 'I just want to cuddle. I just want to watch something and be adored.' But now it feels good, it feels awesome."

SELENA GOMEZ

"Even if I were in a relationship, I'm a single-minded individual, and I really like my freedom. I think there's a lot of people that need to be in relationships and need to be in love. I want it sometimes, but I don't need it."

LIZZO

"Being single used to mean that nobody wanted you. Now it means you're pretty sexy and you're taking your time deciding how you want your life to be and who you want to spend it with."

"**Being single means you're strong enough to wait for what you deserve.**"

NIALL HORAN

"I have not lived as a woman.
I have lived as a man. I've just
done what I damn well wanted to,
and I've made enough money to
support myself, and ain't afraid
of being alone."

KATHARINE HEPBURN

"I'm not alone! I'm with myself. And myself is fabulous."

❤

EVA LONGORIA

"Demographically, single people are more powerful than ever before."

♥

BELLA DEPAULO

"Men are my hobby – if
I ever got married, I'd have
to give it up."

♥

MAE WEST

"I used to think it was important to find a boyfriend, but I don't feel that it is now. I just want to have as much fun and as many adventures as possible."

♥

TAYLOR SWIFT

"I don't need a man to feel whole."

· · · · · · · · · · · · · · · ♥ · · · · · · · · · · · · · · ·

JANE FONDA

2

I'M "THE ONE"

"I've been single for a while and I have to say, it's going really well. Like... it's working out. I think I'm the one."

EMILY HUNTER

"I celebrate myself, and sing myself."

WALT WHITMAN

"Being single is about celebrating and appreciating your own space that you're in."

KELLY ROWLAND

"A man for me is the cherry on the pie. But I'm the pie and my pie is good all by itself. Even if I don't have a cherry."

HALLE BERRY

"If you're not happy single, you're not gonna be happy married."

NICK VUJICIC

"You do not need to be loved, not at the cost of yourself. The single relationship that is truly central and crucial in a life is the relationship to the self. Of all the people you will know in a lifetime, you are the only one you will never lose."

JO COUDERT

"Some of us are becoming the men we wanted to marry."

GLORIA STEINEM

"I know my worth. I embrace my power. I say if I'm beautiful. I say if I'm strong. You will not determine my story. I will."

AMY SCHUMER

3

LOVE YOURSELF FIRST

"If you're comfortable with yourself and know yourself, you're going to shine and radiate and other people are going to be drawn to you."

DOLLY PARTON

"Find the love you seek,
by first finding the love
within yourself."

SRI SRI RAVI SHANKAR

"I was terrified of being alone. Listen, at the end of the day, love is the best thing, but what I've discovered is that I can't get that from somebody else. It's the love inside of me, for myself, that will help me through."

JENNIFER LOPEZ

"Our first job in life as women is to get to know ourselves. I think a lot of times we don't do that. We spend our time pleasing, satisfying, looking out into the world to define who we are; listening to the messages, the images, the limited definitions that people have of who we are."

MICHELLE OBAMA

"Being brave enough to be alone frees you up to invite people into your life because you want them and not because you need them."

MANDY HALE, *THE SINGLE WOMAN: LIFE, LOVE, AND A DASH OF SASS*

"Who are you? Are you in touch with all of your darkest fantasies? Have you created a life for yourself where you can experience them? I have. I am f*cking crazy. But I am free."

LANA DEL REY

"He who knows others is wise.
He who knows himself
is enlightened."

.... 🔷 ....

LAO TZU

"People aren't defined by their relationships. The whole point is being true to yourself and not losing yourself in relationships."

NINA DOBREV

"At the innermost core of all loneliness is a deep and powerful yearning for union with one's lost self."

BRENDAN FRANCIS

"Loving ourselves works miracles in our lives."

················ 👄 ················

LOUISE HAY

"Society's always asking, 'Are you dating anybody?' But I don't think dating is everyone's thing. If you're happy being single, then just be you."

KIM CHI

"I like me very much. When I look in the mirror and my skin glows back at me, I think, 'Wow, that sure is pretty.'"

TINA TURNER

4

SINGLE, NOT ALONE

"You alone are enough.
You have nothing to prove
to anybody."

MAYA ANGELOU

"I used to think that the worst thing in life was to end up all alone. It's not. The worst thing in life is to end up with people that make you feel alone."

ROBIN WILLIAMS

"Too many women throw themselves into romance because they're afraid of being single, then start making compromises and losing their identity. I won't do that."

JULIE DELPY

"I like being single,
I'm always there when
I need me."

ART LEO

"Yes, I'm alone.
But I'm alone and free."

ELSA, FROZEN

"We are complete with or without a mate, with or without a child. We get to decide for ourselves what is beautiful when it comes to our bodies. That decision is ours and ours alone."

JENNIFER ANISTON

"And you scare people because you are whole all by yourself."

LAUREN ALEX HOOPER

"My generation fought very hard for feminism, and we fought very hard to not be labelled as you had to have a husband or you had to be in a relationship, or you were somehow not a cool chick."

STEVIE NICKS

"Discover why you're important, then refuse to settle for anyone who doesn't completely agree."

FISHER AMELIE

"If you really are going to be a happy single, you have to stop treating being single as the annoying time that you pass between relationships and embrace it. Rather than focusing on what you lack, focus on what you have: You."

NATALIE LUE

5

SELF-PARTNERED AND LOVING IT

"I'm a very, very single bitch."

★

LIZZO

"I don't need a man to rectify my existence. The most profound relationship we'll ever have is the one with ourselves."

SHIRLEY MACLAINE

"Your self-worth is determined by you. You don't have to depend on someone telling you who you are."

·········· ★ ··········

BEYONCÉ

"I don't think that because I'm not married it's made my life any less. That old maid myth is garbage."

★

DIANE KEATON

"Of course, I am not worried about intimidating men. The type of man who will be intimidated by me is exactly the type of man I have no interest in."

★

CHIMAMANDA NOGZI
ADICHIE

"Some women choose to follow men and some women choose to follow their dreams. If you're wondering which way to go, remember that your career will never wake up and tell you that it doesn't love you anymore."

LADY GAGA

"You deserve the world even if it means giving it to yourself."

R.H. SIN

"There's something really cool about knowing that your destiny is SO big that you're not meant to share it with anyone. At least not yet."

★

MANDY HALE

"My mother told me to be a lady. And for her, that meant – be your own person, be independent."

★

RUTH BADER GINSBURG

"It took me a long time, but I'm very happy [being single]. I call it being self-partnered."

★

EMMA WATSON

6

THE JOY OF SOLITUDE

"I never found a companion that was so companionable as solitude."

HENRY DAVID THOREAU

"My alone feels so good,
I'll only have you if you're
sweeter than my solitude."

* * *

WARSAN SHIRE

"No partner 'completes' you – you need to be a whole, happy person on your own before sharing your life with someone else."

RUSSELL THACKERAY

"Until you get comfortable with being alone, you'll never know if you're choosing someone out of love or loneliness."

MANDY HALE

"To go out with the setting sun on an empty beach is to truly embrace your solitude."

JEANNE MOREAU

"Why does no one tell us how important it is to enjoy being single and being by yourself?"

DREW BARRYMORE

"**What you are looking for is already in you... You already are everything you are seeking.**"

"The greatest thing in the world is to know how to belong to oneself."

MICHEL DE MONTAIGNE

7

SINGLE PEARLS OF WISDOM

"As a body everyone is single,
as a soul never."

⚡

HERMANN HESSE

"[Marriage] happens as with cages: The birds without despair to get in, and those within despair of getting out."

MICHEL DE MONTAIGNE, *THE COMPLETE ESSAYS*

"Never love anyone who treats
you like you're ordinary."

⚡

OSCAR WILDE

"I think it's very healthy to spend time alone. You need to know how to be alone and not defined by another person."

⚡

OLIVIA WILDE

"He is his own best friend, and takes delight in privacy whereas the man of no virtue or ability is his own worst enemy and is afraid of solitude."

ARISTOTLE

"If your joy is derived from what society thinks of you, you're always going to be disappointed."

MADONNA

"When you are lonely for a while don't get restless. If you had born alone, you are going to die alone then for some time you can certainly live alone."

AMIT KALANTRI

"If we seek paradise outside ourselves, we cannot have paradise in our hearts."

THOMAS MERTON

"Single lady, the man you want might not necessarily be the man you need."

MARTHA MACHARIA

"You're single not because you are not good enough for one, it's that you're too good for the wrong one."

CHRIS BURKMENN

"Being single is definitely better than being with the wrong person."

HASSAN CHOUGHARI

"If we are not fully ourselves,
truly in the present moment,
we miss everything."

THICH NHAT HANH

SOURCES

Bailey, J. 2016. 'Twenty-One Years On, Carrie Bradshaw is Still Teaching Us About Relationships', *Grazia Magazine* [online], www.grazia.com.au – p. 12

Bennetts, L. 2011. 'Olivia Wilde's New Fairy Tale', *Marie Claire* [online] www.marieclaire.com – p. 83

Brine, K. 2017. 'Me, Myself, and The Mountains: Part 2', *Mind Your Mind* [online] www.mindyourmind.com – p. 52

Byng, R. 2018. 'Be Like Ruth: 5 Lessons from Ruth Bader's Early Career Steps', *Forbes* [online] www.forbes.com – p. 66

Byrne, P. 2017. *Double Entendre: The Parallel Lives of Mae West and Rae Bourbon*, Florida: BearManor Media – p. 17

Coudert, J. 1965. *Advice from a Failure*, Stein and Day: USA. – p. 27

DaPaulo, B. 2018. 'There's Never Been a Better Time to be Single', *CNN Health* [online] www.edition.cnn.com – p. 16

Daskal, L. 2014. '65 Quotes That Will Dare You to do Great Things', *Inc* [online] – p. 54

De Klerk, A. 2018. 'Jennifer Aniston on Why She Doesn't Need a Husband or Kids to Fill "a Void"', *Harpers Bazaar* [online] www.harpersbazaar.com – p. 51

Doubts, C. 2017. 'Only the Lonely', *Huffpost*, www.huffpost.com – p. 40